Armed Descent (1961)
Her Body Against Time (1963)
Round Dances (1964)
Enstasy (1964)
Lunes (1964)
Lectiones (1965)
Words In Service (1965)
Weeks (1966)
The Scorpions (1967)
Song XXIV (1967)
Devotions (1967)
Twenty Poems (1967)
Axon Dendron Tree (1967)
Crooked Bridge Love Society (1967)
A Joining (1967)
Alpha (1968)
Finding the Measure (1968)
Sonnets (1968)
Statement (1968)
Songs I-XXX (1968)
The Common Shore (1969)
A California Journal (1969)
Kali Yuga (1970)
Cities (1971)
In Time (1971)
Flesh Dream Book (1971)
Ralegh (1972)
The Pastorals (1972)
Reading Her Notes (1972)
The Tears of Edmund Burke (1973)
The Mill of Particulars (1973)
A Line of Sight (1974)
The Loom (1975)
Sixteen Odes (1976)
The Lady Of (1977)
The Convections (1978)

Editor

A Controversy of Poets (1965)

The CONVECTIONS

Robert Kelly

SANTA BARBARA

BLACK SPARROW PRESS

1978

These poems were composed in 1973, 1974 and 1975. They follow the poems in *The Mill of Particulars,* and share a season with the cycle of *Texts* currently being published in periodicals. Some of the poems have already appeared in magazines, notably *Sailing the Road Clear, The Virginia Quarterly Review, The American Poetry Review, The Muse* and *Poetry Review* (Eric Mottram). The first poem in the book was published originally as a chapbook in 1975 by Helen in Annandale.

ISBN 0-87685-312-2 (paper edition)
ISBN 0-87685-313-0 (signed cloth edition)

TO HELEN

*the best work's
to hear*

TABLE OF CONTENTS

The Convections

THE TEARS OF EDMUND BURKE

Let the ink
run out & return
it is a tide
also
        like the white of its kind,

colorless energy
cloaked in sky,
a queen
on the guillotine
shimmering diamonds

                blade
        of all her falls

glistening in the wet ink.

We fix on Edmund Burke
who saw the young queen
full of beauty & wit,
loved her
as his soul
divided from him by the long
water, the Channel,
the sleeve.
And worshipped her
in tides of ink
so that men said
His politics are amours, his politics are mad,
    he has believed his own words
        & stands dazzled by the diamonds of the Queen
    reflected in his wet ink

white paper
where on sunny days
the prism
throws its manifest,

Burke wept
that his hand was so far from his head,

that his eye was so far from the ink
   & the sleeve on his wrist
would blur the letters when he wrote so fast.

Across the Channel the queen knelt
& lost her head,
diamonds tumbled down & her eyes
reflected light,
Burke could do nothing, his hand
so far from his head.
With the fire of his rhetoric
he heated the forge of his heart,
wept his fluent tears
& formed a crystal of political fact,

      Revolution kills the Woman

he thought, & that is all it does.
"It is the revenge
of men against
all beauty that moved them,
   against words & diamonds
      that made them dance

& they will no longer.
I am the last man

who saw the Queen
dance in her vigor & truth & loveliness,
the flame of her diamonds was harder than Reason

& I have worshipped it
until the end."
He tore his roots up from the earth
& followed her
before the glisten had dried off the ink.

Die every
day & be
born
a little
further on
every
day closer to
form.

We said
we are cursed,
Hyades brought tears,
Pleiades, misadventure :

bright tress of Aldebaran,
distress.

—H.D., *Temple of the Sun*, II.

SAPPHO

Bright tears
huddled in thought,
the curse said
We are alone,

We have no stars.
The hair
streaming as she ran
in all ways
like the sun

showed us a circle
we were,
or were center of,
& all our rapture then

took us from each other
& we ran.

The stars
are our circumference.

15

*

Even as she spoke
her lovers were leaving,
long dresses composed

on their limbs as they went.
That is, melody,
or the drawn lines

sometimes scratched on pottery
to make full
use of the curve,

to reproduce
the drift of their clothes
against them as they ran.

It all
was about going
& being gone.

From the world he took an apple
& chewed it with horses, nights, the eyes
of fieldmice, the skin inside an arm.
His moonlight never faltered, his old
love-affairs also gave light. By them he saw
burnt-out streets filled with dead children,
his own words scribbled on the scorched walls.

He was a loaf of bread. He dropped salt
in the sea & winter came, its clouds
round as any apples, its clouds
gnawed at the house he thought he lived in.
He lived in no house. 'The sky
also has its oil,' he dreamt, 'the hawk
flies down through me when I love her.'

PURITY

A true poem of the eternal present, an ocean, each wave is now, no wave is then. Nothing, comes again.

The reader is no reader. He hears, in one direction, avanti, forever. Not a line, a passage.

This is a truth of process.

For years I hated Lot's wife, who was the Reader Looking Back through the Text. The woman reliving her memories. Rereading the poem.

It must come to this: the line becomes line, as the Word becomes Flesh.

The poem is only when it is. Only the going by right now.

A formal line, of verse, at last breaks down. In a purely serial unfolding, there is no structure possible based on recurrence-within-a-figure.

A line is the breath's take on the heart's grasp of the senses' senses, burnt up in an instant on the altar of the poem.

So the line one hears is an abstraction, sheer guesswork.

The integer of poetic composition is Interruption.

A poem is a controlled interruption of the reader's

associative mental life.

A blank page summons data from the reader's mind. So the page must not be blank, lest the reader's wall never be broken, and he be trapped in the dream-palace of his associative reflections, or if he move out, wander only all day in the vales of Har.

Har is: thoughts without thinking. Concepts without conceiving.

Purity is the other.

So the blank page must have words on it.

ENNEAD 1

Black cloud over white, some snowflakes came
& warmed away. *Gott, welch' Dunkel hier!*
but brightness too. The Gulf Stream changes,
we get wet. "No snow at all below
Portsmouth..." After a week of sixties,
winter comes back. No place for lonely
men, no room for stallions this damp grass.
Let there be no cutting of this root
that here alone strives up out of earth.

Men come after all

this root of earth.

ENNEAD 2

Stanzaic intervention: the dull
craftsman grinds his gouge. I made this line
before, I can do it again, no?
And then the woman came, with her furs
sprawling and her legs too, watched him carve
and said: I know a better wood, come
with me to my country, my old trees
will teach you grain. But he said No, I
dont want to learn, I want to cut wood.

═══════════════════════════════════

Star crafts before,
are legs a country?

Furs carve,
come trees
and sprawl with me
to learn.

ENNEAD 3

Come with me to my country she said
to another. He packed his chisel
and ran at her side. They got there late,
sun was down in the trees, sparrows fell
out of her air. It is strange here now
and she agreed. Here is a table
with food for our supper, eat my share
and when you're done lie down at my side,
I'll show you how to wait for morning.

Late rows fell here
at my side.

Here it is trees.

Try his chisel there:
sun was her air.

ENNEAD 4   (The Elementary Physics Lesson)

Sine is size of wave, is form dead-on,
merry aftermath and part of speech.
White balls made to writhe describe wave-forms
strung on strings, cranked by a teacher's heart
understanding rhythms to his hand.
Amplitude of Natural Philo-
sophy risen from trough of nature's
mind, I see your curves proposing Day —
the green line wavers, turns Horizon.

═══════════════════════════════════════

Scribe,
you trough of Nature's posing!

Speech forms heart-hand.

Balls on strings
writhe by mind.

═══════════════════════════════════════

Verse is Day zone.

ENNEAD 5

Articulate pure vowel sounds for
Mithras; Lord Christ at first was worshipped
that same way — sounds where heart was metric
and a lover's larynx made all Form.
There is no liturgy but our breath —
and a god is what flows out of that
it seems, a space our breath makes happen.
Something answers, some one comes to stand
in that place. Cough up a name for Him.

═══════════════════════════════════════

Where heart was made,
a god is what seems.

Where heart was met,
there is a breath.

ENNEAD 6

Exercise the old sleeper's barn-yard
draggled omniscient hens — one of these
chickens aint no chicken, is *rangé*
or full of grief, how magic works in
from the circumference like an old friend
coming to see you from all sides at
once. Get out and count hens, count cocks, count
stars and grains of millet. He wont sleep
forever, find out before he wakes.

═══════════════════════════════════

See out and ever,
all sides count.
He wont find ever
how like stars
these ran.

*

Mill of grains
and see you full of
stars, come out
and count.
           Or from grief
magic wakes.

ENNEAD 7

Stationed at the gold rim of my sad
planet's orbit send warmth to me and
no more at least for a little while
blasts of formal instruction, lady,
you remember all your days and make
mine out of such recall, let me come
to you straight, right now, no history
but the heat I bring back to you from
the light you send down on my dark bones.

ENNEAD 8

Arch of broken light my bow is strung
of your colors, my house built down out
of your curve. To live on earth is an
exciting destination, a love
affair in this planet hotel. No
life longer than week-end. I hurry,
fumble over every one, I touch
and try to remember. All the while
I get your message from every eye.

_____

Arch of your life-long weekend,
I touch every member,

a love,
no hurry.

Earth is touch.

ENNEAD 9

City beyond the zodiac, flesh
organized at last in meaningful
channels, what goes through the mind is Nile
runs down her legs & looks like serpents
silvering out of darkened arches.
All their song is upright, the head rears,
any word they think of flickers out.
She speaks. Sun rises at the end of
streets. It is because. It specifies.

Flesh means go through.

Song is think

rises because She speaks.

THE LAST RELIGION

and the pier
widened
so that the Dead
in all their difference
could board
that single boat.

CHASTITY

           is a love of not being misunderstood,

    of people at some distance,
                         a 'girdle'
     to preserve,
              a wall enclosing.
Freemason. The wall that walks.
     (And becomes fatuous, as in A Midsommer nights Dreame,
             only when it talks about its hole)

(we have been much too much in holes
   involved with or pursuing, in,)

this wall I will, this garden I am, that moves
   among you, moves by thinking itself there.

Rose is a Hole turned inside out.

On wet black wood Pound saw her petals
   & talked about something else for sixty years
until the acorn opened,
                    clearly, in the sense of Light
& the knowledge
              that light is not vague, is a Defined,
Enclosure)
        a person)
The two Rosie+Crosses:

   the Stavros crowned with seven roses,

   the Crucifixion in the Rose.

KINGSTON, NEAR THE TRAFFIC CIRCLE

Bridge over a river I didnt know
didnt know was there
or where it ran & least
of all its name.

        How songs start
is in a thing seen not seen
before, now held
not with the eyes
          but a shaped breath
comes off the heart
like a wind off the river
& says its name

        1.

          & from these rites together
    a canon of song
or city appears
        (grown west since I last
      saw the lights of it
    almost to the hills now
      in this country where mostly
      a city is flat place
        easy to build
    by the sort of stream
      called river
      for the boast of it
  or they'd dump land-fill
    on the salt creeks

smarter
than climb a hill,
easy
for the Dutch of us)

2.

This river, suddenly, broad
& suddenly there, twinkling
in the new urban dark,

red arrow of Sunoco
pulsing down into its waters,
reflection
of what thought
to show what way?

No way but song
to apprehend
such movements
or sense out
all the way

where these bright garages diners highways arrows rivers go.

WHELPS

of one big
breasted
experience too
large to keep in
sight, only her
young
are with us

can be seen,
today on the hill
by Hogan's old
garage a red
haired boy of six
lifted a red
alder branch
up from the road
as if to let us
pass & he
the keeper of that
turnpike the
common road

or on the hill
down
to Barrytown
a dog
rump in air
worried something
below the ground
& his two
masters, a boy

33

& girl defined
so by the cast
of their shoulders,
her long braided
hair) looked
out over & past
their animal
to the fact of a broad
brown downsloping
field spring
almost upon them.

THE NIGHTMAN

So the wind paled the sky
& the Irish man, no father,
said Let a woman be compared
to a pain in the cock
so that a man can measure

in marriage or merriment
just what it is that comes
to ease him or keep him
away from the world. A bitter
man, not young, not old.

His scarf was rough, he turned
to walk across a field
not his own, a wind
was around him, his road
ran between woman & work

He stuck to it, eyes on the sky.

*'Twas too late to dream of Flying, of Limpid Fountains,
smooth Waters, white Vestments, and fruitful green Trees...*

—Sir Thomas Browne, *A Letter to a Friend*, 17.

The man hurries to his death through a maze of dreams.

He hurries his circle like a hoop
     hit moving along the path,
             jounces
on the ill-kept brick walkway in his garden,

he hurries his dreams.
      "Have you no time
      for us or to hear us?"
           his dreams cried,

but he ran faster through them,
spat them out of his waking mind,
       ran
through the doorway to the strange bed
felt the woman, her warm deep
peculiarity, roundness, he cried out
what he could not name, became.

A MY NAME

When we were children, the girls sang a counting game and jump-rope game chant:

> *A my name is Alice / my husband's name is Andrew /*
> *we come from Alabama / and we sell apricots.*

Tremendous stress on the last word, APRIcots. And so on through the alphabet. It was to be seen how far she could go, always and instantly coming up with a new name, a new husband, a new homeland, a new commodity, all alliterating. So our ears were trained in rhythm, how to fit the names in of different lengths, a living demonstration of the vitality of Measure and the impuissance of meter, that trivial mitre-box. Cradle of surrealism: any alliterating name would work, but only the wilder or dirtier or more wonderful ones elicited a ripple of delight from the girls standing around waiting their turn, from the boys clustering close, to hear and see all they could of this mystery.

The game chant taught this: that reality is polar, male-female, tantric. That to be entitled to be at all, you needed a wife (a husband). That you are defined by your place. That you've got to have some product, the stranger the better. That the product should have some affinity with your identity. That you've got to bring it all to market. That it all has to come to market.

This chant was my first news of the Great Trade Route along which scarce and isolate merchant-poet-nomads carried the goods from tribe to tribe, over the mountains and under the sun, bringing the only news.

37

SPIES

Guys in trees
subtracting branches
so wires wont snarl.
We're all plugged
in series, tangled
with a destiny
looks like a phonebill
unpaid on the floor
getting stepped on
but the numbers always
unfortunately clear.

*

The trained cormorant
lights on every house,
Watson, the *picche* also,
Dante's jackdaws, Watson,
mascots of our greed.

*

Hot morning after a week of sun,
all the lake roses or pink
stand out for heat,
                     laic
(order of laymen) somewhere
a breeze (a hierarchy)
through the republican haze.

*

"My testimony
is compelled. I do this
at your command,
across the coffee cups
on the terrace, women
in their bright clothes
going up and down the stairs.
Ghirardelli Square."

There he rested, drank
drab coffee, smoked,
watched his convictions
dissolve in the elegant air.
This was no place to have opinions —
any minute she'd
be back from the john
and then he'd have
to talk again, show interest.

"But a cloud got to me
before she did,
I was up
in the sky now
watching my body wait
and her body come along
with firm honest sexual tread
to join him — now
I was gone, now over the Bay
seeing nothing but its steel water
subtly shifting,
the iris sheen of gasoline.
Hours later, among the eucalyptus,
I came down with the rain."

A PASTORAL ITEM

My circuits fill
with the pink-noise
that is Sabbath
when folk are free to drive,
        arrive,
interview oak trees & caress
        public castles,
remark the humidity, drink.

Old Sabbath was resting place
but New a journey,
                    there is no patience
    in this discothèque,
sad old things shake under the shuffle.

So I give you three sheep
we saw hurried down the road
by an accurate pebble-throwing shepherd –
they jumped through the hedge
as we passed
because we drove so slowly
that they noticed us,
                    first one
who bolted, then the other two,
then the first backed out,
jumped in again
where the others
crashed through to safety,

sheep masks in sumac.

WASPS

I stood at the window cursing wasps
because they fell for the same tricks;
the light *(Mehr Licht!)* was thick,
they thought it glory but it was prison
because they believed in it. He
worshipped its color. But the light
persisted in its mystery, was question
not answer, effect not cause.
More light! Goethe called, but *No
light,* the Rabbis knew, *No light at all.*

THE HOURS

I thought of the strata of time
through which the animals
still take possession of our places.
All day long the lordly stupid dogs
bold as boyars strut and drone;
and when they doze the jewish cats
come in — what looks so feminine is fear,
self-possession, silence, dread of change.
Towards night the birds appear again
and thieve till darkness. Then the dog
hobbles his estate again, spoiling
what he does not use. Now
the mouse allowed and expert skunk,
and after midnight the raccoon.
All after our seeds and garbage,
all taking their places in the hours
until at the bottom of the dark
the oldest comes alone, opossum.

12 August 1973
for Helen

A MEETING IN HYPERBOREA

The party for the Pole
found him on an icefloe
reading *The Northern Bee*
with the latest Dostoevsky
sent in by astral flyer,
Reindeer Express, pressed
out in ice & haste & fire,
battle of the elements
against
       the interruptions
       human order makes
in the true-gold-washed haughty
brilliance of the cosmos,
                "We are alloys!"
he shouted at the sledge.
But our captain denied it,
pointed to the dancing
crackle on the oscilloscope
& said All purity is sine-wave,
we are *vinum merum,*
only the bravest angel drinks us down.
A gulp or sob
starts in the voice.
A smile
       offered to us from the ice,
a sideways masochist grin,
his feet are clearly cold,
all the pages he's turned
cant keep him warm.

[So I think about the hot bright

highway to Hyde Park,
warmth of my skin
as I walk to Stockenberg's
for an AC plug & a pair
of needle-nose pliers
as if I were a man on earth.
Special on screwdrivers,
I love this place,
out to the hot street.
Helen's smiling in the car,
drug store a success,
town patrolcar waiting to pull
out behind her, an old woman
waiting to pull in.
Lovely smell in the car, Italian
oil of bergamot, drive south,
nach Süden]

              Why
stand a hundred years on that ice
when by learning
forty-odd phonemes
you could return
or come for the first time
to the American town —
no girls today in the soda shop,
none sitting outside on the sidewalk
as they usually do
in contact with chthonic mysteries,
no priests in the churches,
no Luthers, no movies, the news
stand closes first,
the last bus of the day is gone.
Go, come back here

from your arrogant snow,
land of cocaine,
                    chinese rhapsodes,
red hot peppers.
World Artist,
this is my lens!
Through which I see nothing
but the sexual charms
of ordinary life,
                    sex is that country
                    where any is every.
Land of Cockaigne.

"I slept my life away
then woke on a floating island,
my feet were cold, the only
talk I had was birds."
Then come back with us
to the enterprise of ordinary life
but he said "No,
I have no name at least,
no need for your
whatever they are —
it's my funeral
& my cold feet.
By now the birds have women's voices
& that will do me
for conversation.
Depart my wilderness
but leave a handkerchief
if you can spare one —
I eat no longer, drink
what rains into my mouth only,
but once a year I cry."

They left him there, the silk
bandanna dropped at his feet.
Was it Judas? The monster
made by Frankenstein? King Arthur?
It was no one
                whose name they knew,
        a man from nowhere
who stayed there
        against all the drunk or sober somewheres
those white men held in their hearts.

THE ETRUSCAN SUN

(Susan and her friend Joseph slept in a farmer's field north of
Rome. She dreamt the sun was rising red, but when it rose
fully into the sky, it turned to stone. In the morning, they
found they had slept among the ruins of an Etruscan temple.)

What was the heart of her story,
tired, on their bicycles, night

coming on while they tried to reach
Lago di Balseno, the farmer,

his permitted field, earth under,
north from Rome, her dream?

The sun rose twice, once of fire
once of stone. Then a third time,

morning over the fields, round house,
ruins, temple, the unknown gods.

                              *

The field is always permitted,
isnt it, and the sun allows us

to look at its transformations.
She said it was the way a sun

rises in, or is seen from, Manhattan,
splendor filling empty streets,

bright key come into the lock,
redness. Then fully in the sky

turned as if the wrong way. To lock
the world. Sun turned stone.

The archaic metaphor takes flesh.
It was grey. Grey like ordinary stone.

*

I had thought the sun she saw
might have been cooked earth, brown

of Etruscan pots and statuary.
But it was grey stone. The color

of morning had gone from it
but there was still enough light

for her to see what it became.
Stone risen out of her dream.

*

How tired they were, trying for a lake
before sunset, to camp there.

But night came on. The farmer
permitted them to rest in his fields.

Why did she, telling the story,
make so much of that permission?

Because any vision must grow
up from ordinary life,

be faithful to its roots (minutes,
dollars, kilometers)? How tired

she was from cycling. Permission
let her sleep into the dream.

*

Has it been that way all ways,
big eyes of the Etruscans, amber,

terra cotta, their eyes had all the colors
and the world a stone lit by a stone?

Stone of mystery to which our passion turns,
flagrant above horizon — is that

a betrayal of our powers, relaxing
of the colors we were meant to shine

out from ourselves always, all ways?
Her eyes were amber,

she had come from the east to see this,
as the sun had. The two of them.

*

Be kind to me, I meant, and
thank you for the dream, I said.

49

These things are given, arent they,
to pass along, a message or mystery.

That the lost language be solved
by the stone that's left,

only the stone,
and these things rise, dont they,

above the personal horizon
into a sky we share. A sky

we are, I meant, our heat
the heart of it.

A CANTICLE FOR JOHN BAPTIST

Was it *voluntary*, to die in the woman's dance?
Wrongs that make a right?
From the forgotten spaces in the story
did I hear *another* dancing
     fog up the hill, dirty fog
     rim of snow around
high fortress, even winter, high choice
to accept that dance
as signal of my own transcendence
and part, leaving my body
to the snowy earth and fetching my head,
my eyes still filled with her dance,
to the land from which the light falls
that makes her shadow,
                  she lifts me in her hands?

She cut me
from contingency
now I
am the sun
to ray down on her, or rise in her
through her anger, she dances
more in anger than in lust,
her thoughts far away
from her delirious body
               deliver me from mine
into an anger that is forgiveness,
why?
     that I had to die
parcelled in her ecstasy
and my ascent become
the proper kingdom to which her dance must bring her.

And Venus was the character of this civil beauty, which the physicists later took for the beauty of nature, and even for the whole of formed nature, as being beautifully adorned with all sensible forms

—Vico, *New Science*, 689

Say I looked in a river and saw myself there
erratically constant, reflection
of the light reflecting from my hidden face,

say this city a notorious *we* have constructed
is the shape of our hearts and gapped
as they are with crimes and failures and forgets.

'Civil beauty!' Extraordinary, passionate
combination of words, each chill, together
twinned like firestick and socket, blazing—

not metaphor! Beauty is city.

WAKING TO HAYDN

Sun bright on powder snow,
unnumbered. The classic style
never further than the mind away.
When the mind had heart.
And what have you? Tonality
will always come back.

(They were wrong in thinking 'melody' the equivalent of
'representation' in the eyes' arts. Melody insists not as image
does but as space does, in all its size. Scale of attention.

The only equivalents that need concern us are structural. The
pattern on the carpet, yes, but the carpet is on the floor, a
room, sunlight comes in and treats not all parts of the pattern
the same.)

*

What would the music treat
                    or treat the same?
                                        a fall
            from high places,
                        to restore men
                to their original lowliness with god
at the foot of the letter?
                        First the word.
                                    No classic
urge.
        Satie tells it, the brass frog
that dreams all night
                    of the insects asleep in its mouth.

Hieroglyph of this unfallen world
caressed around our fall —

we fell
on sleep, mere sleep and all its dream.

*

So stretched on his bed he resolved to make no more differ-
ence between what he called sleep and what he usually called
being awake. Let all of that, turn and turnabout, be called
sleep. Then there must be (he knew, as the rumor of that
space instantaneously enlarged around him) both another wa-
king, and also a deeper dream. All his life he'd crept along
the rind, neither leaping off the fruit of the world nor in fact
deeply eating it.

Or climb Boot Hill. Where the dead bury their dead. Where
the dreams climb to sleep in their own turn.

When a man goes to sleep, it is a woman wakes.

THE TEMPLE

This little place
sacred to the singular,
bathroom
where in this
American house
a child's alone
& only there.
And here
he takes
his body for the whole of him,
loves his holes
as secret gates of wonder.
Place of water,
touch of it to know,
the skin,
fire & air, secret
smokes of his inner
breath released
at last, blue plumes
around his nostrils,
earth of his
most sacred dung,
wisdom-temple —

if people are never alone
then this is Alone
& what they do with it —

He lights a cigarette
& smokes it too fast,
incense-offering

to Agnî, puffs,
sees himself in the mirror,
the mind & the mirror
his only Rig-Veda.
He feels creation
shuddering below,
strips off his clothes
to press against cold tile —
this is my body,
this hard cold knows me,
touches me.
House of sensation.
To feel is to be.
He squats on the toilet,
lets the inner mass
press gently out,
feels his control
to speak this too,
releases. A stir
of fire at the root,
smoulder
around his base —
this is no yearning
but a being.
He is alone here.
There is no woman
in this place, the harlots
of his mind
press out through his skin
his hands on his body,
alone, no society
will let him in,
every world
is boring, talky,

fleshless.
He wipes
himself reverently,
strokes the closed gates,
stares down in the vessel
where his dung floats.
He pisses on it now
carefully, drops the
cigarette in.
Offerings mingled in the cup
he flushes away
into the sacrificial waters —
Go under earth,
ripen,
restore.
The chalice cleans
itself again.
                    Now
he rests his face his mask
against the cool mirror
that warms from him,
from his soft breath.
His closed eyes
shyly open,
look
into his eyes.
He is no one.

EPONA

mare; horsehead elevated Queen;
of whom Bottom; in the assnoll is
a proper servitor; list, not syntax?

passion not thought? I will arrest
the operation; of my passion;
for the sake of the operant; who

is mare-withered; maned;
marely big-rumped; strong;
whose children run along

beneath her; beside her;
they are the harriers; the hunt;
their hurry; is geological;

what they course over takes their shape,
is land; hill; ravine & lake;
her only they pursue; who;

that we are inhabitants; of a space
she & her kind; shaped;
so to move at all; is worship her;

& hurry! with articulate deeds;
to seize her traces; to recede;
to primitive enthusiastic condition,

to be wild; to call her; Epona; Ekwona
damsel of horses; midden maiden;
not maid; mad mother genuflect

only weary, for water; to stumble;
I have followed; you all this hasty day;
hid in your body's; shadow; you drink.

OF VALENTINE

for Helen

what I heard
looking
out over this
sprawled snow hill
into the dawn
a fine cracked
sky lightening
through the gap,

that is to say letting
some light in.

*

That is to say looking it up:

"at Rome, on the Flaminian Road, in the time of Emperor
Claudius, the birthday of Saint Valentine, priest and martyr,
who after having cured and instructed many persons, was
beaten with clubs and beheaded"

*

Sappho tells it also,
beaten, my body beaten
as with rods (for Love)
I lost my head for Love
and other stratagems
left to lurk in the joke

2.

Claudius?
Could he?

Road of the *flamens*,
cognate with brahman,
our word might be blagman or blawman
sacrifice-priest,
who knows the score
by heart.

      It is this heart
      today is lost,
         the sense of it,
    a picture of a fine fat heart
    shapely as a woman's ass upside down,
         sent to your love
  color of cherry, this heart that is point & delve,
         cherry, acorn of the cock
  lifted,
         the head of it we say, lifted
towards Love,
         as the blawmen would lift the fire now,
    sun disk not over Briggs' pasture yet

& set it on the hard stinking stone
left over from so many offerings so
many dreams now
         to clean it try to clean it
one more time in the face of this skeptic dawn

3.

Today is to lose our hearts to
but not lose heart,
lose our heads to
but not our heads —

I would want to hear
the voice of this Valentinus
whose birthday
(they mean deathday)

a very old tradition
says this is,
        I mean to hear
it from his mouth
exactly

whom he cured & what
instructed, in the name of
Love was it?, as I have
many times been myself

cured & instructed by Love.
I want a testimony out of a man's mouth
not an old tradition,
I mean I want a friend not a book,

yet here is where the earth
most lets itself be quiet,
that so few men, lovers or it may be
not lovers at all, did or do

concern themselves with this work
of opening their mouths —
I need a word from Valentinus
who died or was born

in such a way, beaten with clubs,
sinewed with thin fire, trembling
of my hands even in cold morning,
beheaded, headed off,

that we take it to be or be
about Love.

4.

So this heart wont work, this emblem,
pretty as the ass is, hot as red is,
wont work
                because it wont talk

& we have invented brain
to strongbox our thoughts & as
we must call them feelings
but of Valentine himself
what I hear is credible,
head lost, beaten
with rigid intentions,
who cured & instructed
must in the fact
of that, that alone,
have been the lover
I would walk out to greet
now, even lighter,
coming over the fields
with his head or his heart in his hands
saying something I can understand.

THE HEAVENLY COUNTRY

Once I thought it was the place my father brought me and my mother to, between the rivers up north. The near river was full of white stones bleached in the sun, and the banks on the far side were red clay. At night it was almost cold, so we slept with blankets or walked out in sweaters early morning to see deer or whatever else might reveal itself to us. That it is a matter of It willing to reveal to Us I have never doubted.

Later I thought it was England. Perhaps only tonight, in my thirty-ninth year, have I been able to bear up under a sort of intellectual scrutiny and realize that it is not England. Till now, all the paradises seemed green places in which words like weir and stream and wood and moor and fell and rain and sheep and cloud and hill might accurately be spoken. It was Tolkien's England after it was De la Mare's England after it was Chesterton's England after it was Kipling's England after it was Doyle's England after it was Kilvert's England, Hopkins' England, Wordsworth's England, Blake's England. Always the shire and the sure, the comfortable man-sized landscapes, cool summers, a shimmer of rainy light to hold us closer in the known.

What I am writing is a confession. I saw those vistas with the wilful eye of protracted Innocence. Winnie the Pooh was closer to my heart than *Christabel*, and to say so is to confess myself not a child but a divided man who has trifled with visions of degradation and visions of exaltation without admitting either to the center of my heart. So I suppose now that center to be not known, and I flounder as I floundered thirty years ago, in shy love of a country innocent and personal as a piece of bread in my mouth, and like it silent, comforting, warm and selfish.

When Blake spoke of Satanic mills, I refused to think of the Manchester my great-grandfather came from, that Engels so passionately anatomized: I thought instead of mythologies, and ahrimanic intensities lathing cogwheels for the heart. I thought always outside of town, except for Baker Street, which was alive (remember) with rain and fog and wind, but only one person at a time. The sexy women of actual England, Mollies and Nell Gwynnes and Christine Keelers, inhabited a different chamber of my thought, along with the Rochesters and Aretinos and Sades: an international of the flesh that, for all my concern with it, had nothing to do with any England at all. There were no Scarlet Women among Owl's relations.

It hardly troubled me that the men who seemed to know the place best were troubled by a lust or dread that wormed their hearts; I took the summer glow of Machen's garden and left his ægipans and troglodytes alone, left Hardy's anguish and Lawrence's need to be answered, and contented myself with the storms and trees and birds and small furry animals hardly consequential to their histories.

Certainly I needed the place. Perhaps I even used it well, husbandman of a land I've never entered. I think those intimate landscapes lie behind my perceptions and registrations of nearer or 'realer' country; sometimes they show through, when yearning or demand overpowers me looking at, say, the big field down Barrytown with the mountains low beyond it. Not this field, the mind whispers, but a field just like it somewhere else, no lovelier at all, but *there*.

Now tonight I give the mind its *there*, but force it to its work.

Not England, not even England at another time (some May morning between Robin Hood and Malory). Not the sheep and not the rock, not the richness of that well-watered grass, the grey sky perfecting all the colors of earth. Not that, but what *that* in turn resembles or shadows. Now, mind, do your work. Find the country whose present nearby shadows I have so long mistaken for no better thing than its shadows somewhere else. Find the there to which all I have ever known or dreamt or fantasized is here.

This night that unlocks England, and keeps me from worshipping the shadow of a shadow, may it unlock too all the chambers of my heart, all the places I've too long protected from reality. By that word I mean whatever that true country or condition is this field puts me in mind of.

Who will claim
this lame lover
feeling along the music
like a blind animal
to come to her body
from which he hears it flow?

Men make music in her shape
(I tell him) & that is why
we call it music, shaped
in craft to resemble women.

He ignores my explanations.
He goes right along
fumbling towards her
for the music's sake
or her sake he cant
tell them apart.
It is the only
honesty I understand,
to persist that way, to go.

THE BEACH AT SUNKEN MEADOWS

Rough sand stone cold
this finely divided music
blue mussel, purple
shells of the limpets
cling to rocks
Helen gathers,
a woman gathers,
beauty of her this
morning in a purple gown
comes back now in the wet
crimson inward of the shell.
Off east three girls are sitting
crosslegged in the sand,
it will rain soon, I cant hear
their voices but I feel
by the magic of this rock
the firm pressure of
their bodies transmitted
from cold sand into the air
of this deserted beach on earth,
they read the tides
or make the tides or Helen
in them patrols her shore
where the Sound breaks
around the cliffs & runs
in very softly very cold
around my feet I watch the
current lower out of sight.
In this rock, this finely
divided, this sand. Later
the girls run on land, away,
I interpret their hips as they run

like bird cries, bird passes
low over the sunken meadows
inland a few hundred yards.
And up behind me out of the grey
loom the coasts of America itself
of which all my life is
only a foretaste, as seeing these
girls run in the wind
is a foretaste of Helen
when the rain comes to land
and the night allows us.

The pears
all week
on the icebox
I never ate

promising myself
every day
they would be
riper

A T'ANG TRAVELER WRITES HOME

Finding my way south
through the gates
my eyes make
of any new place

to the horrible hot country
where men mate with
beasts or trees
& their children whine

all afternoon
flies at their eyes,
the swamp's bad air
waiting for me —

I would prefer then
a mineral condition
to impart my presence
to a worthwhile rock

or cluster of limestone
pinnacles, ruins
as it were of some
unknown house

up out of the very green
rainforest. I have crossed
no line but I have come
beyond intention

into a jungle war once
more. I defer
all responsibilities
except to this stone.

NEWTON

Eternity here, beginnings and the fortunate
end compacted in a minute, I look
out at the sombre trees on this cool May evening
when the air is very still, between the seasons
when the woman I have addressed and been answered by
so long stands up from beside the hearth
and with a last stir given to the cauldron says
   Come and taste this garden we have brewed
   from the water of Thales and Plato's roots,
   it was never easy, it is almost done, let us
   taste it together.
               That's how the night begins,
this nycthemeral presentation of the world
beyond the senses we are given we are given.
I stand beside her and in the first taste
remember the thousands of years of effort
to clarify the water, not a word is left to tell it,
but the taste tells, and then those solids
Plato recovered from the ones lost before him
that they had rooted
              out of the air, perfected or
more truly *saw* the complex perfections
of air going to fire, earth going to air
going to fire, water under earth going to
air going to fire.
          How many of them was I?
And does this man who remembers himself in the taste
and speaks with my tongue
            speak
               from any more interesting
or accurate place, not experience,

experience tells nothing we can use, a place,
is there a place from which I can
here make an entry
                    that you can hear me, see me
in all the continuous excitation of the senses,
images
        sheared out of the spaces which are no place,
image of the place which is no space?

"He very rarely went to bed till two or three of the clock
sometimes not until five or six, laying about four or five
hours, especially at spring and fall of the leaf, at which times
he used to employ about six weeks in his elaboratory, the
fires scarcely going out either night or day."

UNDER THE FLASHING MOUNTAIN OF HEAVENLY IRON

Let the letters be drawn clear
at last on that rock
     candy cloud bedewed mountain, wandering
Rock with a hot heart & so many tongues
I swear it I couldnt count.
But it is true that the women are worse than the men,
they talk more, say more, report
through the garble of cloud this thing they know, one by
one of them, no them, she
       in fact does know this, speaks
& so compassionately with such sweetness & the smell of her hair
also compelling me
     compels to discourse,
         of which this is language
& a good part, the bones of thought
      but my thinking is another anger
not as slow as to say.

    The instruments are still on hand at the slope,
talus, the insecure power of what had assumed stability
only to coerce me from the enraptured amplitude
of wandering caress, whereby I had been all over & all
under
   so came up here out of India to cram it in a cave.
Just past the swamp country, in the flex of Brahmaputra,
there came into my heart the thought to bespeak these people
dripping sweat into their milpas & shaking with fear of
what seemed to me priests,
      & assort them of the variety of the one
particular I had found necessary to favor,
        a knowing that was

itself at once epistemon & coitus. So I spoke
                                    out, in their
nearness, & they did themselves the honor of listening.

I am a Mean Flower, I said, cantankerous, persistent, but as well
the middle term between something & nothing, between thinking
                                             & thought
& I have chosen to spur in your overwatered earth
                                        to assure you
that there is a condition which is not conditioned.
                                        That is knowing.
And I invite you to consider
                    this knowing, as I have known to know,
& you will find it
                    both a bed & a road & in either employment
a sweet coming & going at once. You will find it a fuck,
I assure you.

        I picked a rock up from the slope
to illuminate my discourse, This is hard you suppose, &
crushed it so that the falling grains exhibited
the pattern of a swallow falling from my hand
before they distributed themselves on the chaff of the threshing
                                                    floor
I stood on to address them & showed no pattern at all.

SERMON TO THE SANGHA AT KAILASA

[After the alert
the hosts of the remnant
premembered their future again
& huddled violently
in towards that rhythm of perception
or time of their minds
which from the beginning had been their City,
demonstration of their function
set up in a level plain.
                        A shadow it threw down
almost to the shores of the lake
where the custodians of civic pleasure
wearing long sheer dresses like apsarases
controlled the shimmering early summer rain.
There the fruit trees were,
                        & rowboats docked
in rows of blue & green,
                        some few out on the lake
where women & consorts fished for reflections.
Not an easy time. The war had come & gone
& come again & would not certainly go away.
From dawn to twilight, Workers
were busy at the Catalogue, ordering, ordering,
while the few who were chosen Legates of the Day
went out slantwise from their perceptions
into the unseen world.
                        Trembling notebooks.
They hurried home & wrote down what they could
too fast, too completely, their hands
terrified of manumission.
                        It all

could be forgotten & their work done –
but the world would go with them, the City
they could never betray would crumple back
to an ordinary convolution in the cerebrum,
locked in the calvarium,
                              the prisonhouse.]

                              *

Unseen, not missed by our slavemasters,
we have gathered by this simple lake
because traditions tell us it is holy.
That is a pious & reasonable persuasion
but it will not help us. We have written
what can be written, spoken what we have heard
speaking in the immense spaces we mistake for our minds.
Up now, into the forgetful air
that thinks itself a condition or grace
but is only the wind of our passage.

Tantra is deed:
                    a song in action
which premembers
                    & constitutes anew
the structures of void
where to meet is the same as no meeting
& the joy of the lake is not different from the Catalogue
& the hand is not different from what it writes down
& the war goes out like a candle in an empty house.

The lore is Davidness,
a dance around the table
where the octave breaks
like the word *affection*
in the throat of a boy
not quite fourteen, him-
self slender perhaps strong
& minded (& more than
minded) to dance in honor
to approach Her whose
pronouns elude him
steadily,

   breaks & the scale
goes up as words & down as
his body, the first one's,
dances to the east.

   He had
a good grandfather, this one,
& a father who told him
Earn but dont save, Love
but dont even try to possess,
Trust no knowledge that does not
continually remember itself in you.
With such instruction even
at the altar's end when west's
the only way to go he runs
there also lightly, not plodding,
not fated, until the stone

is content to accept him
as its lord, as he in his time
comes to know her as the coil
inside which he moves
now but will at the end of his life
break out from with a sudden
overwhelming grace.

AN ORIGIN

[from a third century papyrus]

for Helen

from an oak took bright
   and warmed it in the sun
  evidently honey, work of the dewloving bee
     wove all day around the god's head
  and filled the hollow of the tree
     with its intricate work
                  now the sun
    broke down the obsessive cells
  to make the honey, natural from outside this
System
     flow like oil,
         and the wax flowed too
     so Pan
  his hairy arms by now all sticky
could glue his reeds together with the wax
         held when cool, evening,
     his pipes
   lined up from long to short
      skyline
    of a city he had founded
   receding infinitely from his touch
         to the last lipped note
when later he tried it;
       and like the bee around him danced
  one other industrious feminine
  a Bacche girl, she pranced

79

                    all round him
              wanted his pipe in her mouth,
                 may have meant to steal it
              to dance her dances with
                              and Pan
                 touched it not too gentle to
              just the edges of her lips
                              she blew
           and he recovered his instrument
                              with his own mouth
       and breathed into it with power or skill
                              such that his body
                 stiffened with the effort
                    and the muscles of his torso tensed
                 as only the sound poured
                              out and down
                    frightening the girl a little
                 then the sound
                              hung in her ears as she
       rushed to the place of her proper dance
                              and later,
                 remembered,
                    was music.

                              80

THE ACQUISITION

I saw the web resplendent strung
in the crotch of a prostrate baytree
so what little sunlight filtered down
through redwoods found its way here,
to be proclaimed & multiplied on the strands
moulded by a small body, its house & instrument.
As a brave American I tried to possess it,
doing deft things with my camera
& duly months later had the stigmata
on a nearby wall: a spiderweb slung
in almost perfect focus, a glimmering
pond of standing water just behind.
Several angles, good shots, I forgot
the spiderweb & its business with the light,
I had collected an experience.
I had shared the spider's feast.

Now today in the first warmth of June
I haul this memory out, delicate, damaged
by two years in the generalizing mind
& try to reconstitute it between me
& the powdery sky. No such gothic lights,
an altogether gentler condition than California.
And by the calmness of the air I find myself
compelled to understand this web afresh
as evidence of the self's power to cast
its thought as physics in a physical world,
spin matter & consent to live in it.
But I am unfair to the spider, who has the power
to leave this cloth she's spun, resorb
her productions in her self again & travel
along straight lines difficult for us to credit
across the light & find another intersection
waiting at the end of herself for her to become.

RAIN

He is not always attentive,
sometimes he sleeps
dreaming simply of women,
                great buildings,
                    a marine city
                mountains
            & certain graceful human
                    bodily acts
from which he wakes refreshed.

He tries to attend.
He says his dreams aloud
and they become day.

2.

Color is the something of anything,
& of it more has been posited than known.

It is not always even bright. Even always bright

colors lose a certain edge from frequency.
And colors are frequencies

but the colors he is trying to talk about here
are those perceptible
all at once in a grey cool rainy midday,
but individually knowable
only one by one as the stations of the process passing
outside the often overcast windows of the One Work.

3.

The veil
is hers

he draws
it round him.

It is old
& he is aging,
it is thick
warm & substantial,
Irish, thornproof,
woven in a house,
smoked in its hearth.

He too is Irish,
he remembers
the rough tough tweed
when it was pale
diaphan

          but it changes
with its ocean.

Its colors
arise between
her & her changes.

The veils
are hers.

4.

Rain,
that simple root

he ravined up
& left the sentence bare

until it dawned
in him,

one could be close
to being close

so he said it again
having heard it the first time:

O rain
you simple root

you
who have always arrived.

FIRST OCTOBER MEDITATION

Out here in the clement late morning of the sun
not yet to full noon have come
the imperious gestures of humankind, not yet
past this phase I examine between my feet sometimes
needling my ankles, the kittens, Man-
and-Woman thou art, scrabbling up the carton
meaning to fall if a day might come when
the sun for a moment stands at noon.
      But noon is no stand, no dig, no dyke.
It passes like a shiver then the hair lies down
to the ordinary condition. Noon means:
Orgasm in the cosmos come to earth.
"The long upward twist
of wet bodies from my wetter dreams spilled
out into the domestic world, Satan was born
& all his Naiades he trains
to turn me on and turn away — Alberich I'm."
No public or historic Nixies. Those girls
were goals exclusive to his private mind,
slipped up on shore, he woke & grabbed,
they left a slick trail. That way the music
followed — or rather the first note of it
alone did follow & all the rest
had to extrude itself to push ahead
that bell-note wandering sheep-starved
woman hungry E! to wrap around them, to take hold.
      He never. So I sit here forgiving
girls that passed for ghouls & goals
that flowed back under the carpet,
under the doorsill where the angry sea
kept patient with an effort. Poor Alberich.

85

Poor skinsick tyrants lecherous for touch.
Poor therapeutized middle-class. Poor hand
that has such pressure on it
to make contact and that be paradise.

SECOND OCTOBER MEDITATION

for Helen

It is the end of October the flies
even the flies are getting desperate
it will be Scorpio any minute & what then?
I watch the flight pattern the fly pattern
Bu kız çok güzel is the sentence I am concerned with
but the flight pattern goes right past me
& unfolds before me like Picasso
painting with a glowing cigarette
on the emulsion locked behind a focused open-eyed camera
pictures I saw once in *Life*. They looked
like Aurignacian oxen or did *Life's* nameless commentator
say: how much like Aurignacian oxen Picasso's are,
these bulls and cows and other oxen? Aurignacian?
Bu kız çok güzel, that girl is pretty,
that udderless cow gives no milk, the girl
is pretty, Picasso did not take her
there in front of the camera with his cigarette,
I am left with my Turkish sentence & my doubt:
what if he did her? what if he took that
pretty Turkish girl & did her so her picture
would unfurl as uninterrupted journey of light
across the coalsack of the emulsion, a face & arm
uplifted, a body bent to earth only to swivel
up from the momentary touch & be graceful
between things or behind them, a woman, a picture?
What if? And if what? *Many mosques*, the grammar says,
How many mosques? How many glasses of water?
It is that way with October, that the sun
kindled this morning after some cold days
so here at 1:30 it is almost 60 yet Helen
picking up milk bottles stored by the garden wall

to wash & return finds
ice in one of them despite the sun, long night,
the long dark growing longer with lines of light in it
spun by Picasso his bulls and cow-like women
imitated now by a late October fly
desperate to get in somewhere for winter, to mate
& make many before the austerity of the year.
I watch the fly pattern the flight pattern
strung across the screen across the sky utterly blue
the leaf-copper rustling ruin of the ash the linden
it will be Scorpio any night now & what then
when the seminal waters arise to breed against winter
to make many before the beautiful annihilating One
comes & beats her white wings against the window.
How many girls are pretty? how many of those girls?
how can I get inside? the fly is the pattern he flies
the fly is he flies, it is only the quickness of time
that keeps me from seeing every picture he draws
on the emulsion of my mind but my mind knows
doesnt it, how many leaves & how the fly flies
& how pretty the girl is & how many glasses of water?

THIRD OCTOBER MEDITATION

At the back of my mind I hear a muted conversation
only a few words come through, broken into strange
haunting pieces, "benefactors of the race," "niche
in time or eternity," "a place, a place to serve."
In front of my eyes the 29¢ turkey-backs
drip garlic & grease from the rotisserie.
The meat turns slowly on the long spit, the rotor
grinding, once every revolution it growls
into low gear & goes up hill. I get tired of hearing
so I listen, get tired of that so come outside
where the cats are nested on foamrubber fallen
frequently from my chair. Porch in shadow,
mild day, as if the sun lay on her side on the mountains
& lifted her skirt to show the eastern fields
glowing in her natural light: this is earth, this is
Time itself, the normal, the unconfused
to which all your prestidigitations
do not finally produce a convincing answer.
Atheist sun. I wish I could hear what I'm thinking,
but those voices in the backroom know their time,
a different sort of scale, they know the when & why.
The how's in my hands, soft friendly capable fingers
numb from all the prestidigitatorlessnesses
this secular world contrives us. I look out above them
at that ostensibly simple field, feminine light oh yes,
oh yes the comings & the comings again, they stir
back behind the flimsy chipboard wall, pons, head
& the mind behind it full of twitter
from which those occasional words in sequence,
"fierceness," "change your life," "your life
is given in eternity to combat time," "time
is your enemy, benefit the race, aggress, address

89

this world as not this woman, rise."
Against time. Against time or its arrant emblems
these dimwit fingers anxious for the cold,
these spilling leaves. I can, I can.

FOURTH OCTOBER MEDITATION

Can I capture the sound of rain in the drainpipe
if the typewriter hums between words & thoughts?
What is there between words & thoughts worth capturing?
Is it the sound of hurrying to the ground,
sign of an element between water & fire?
The sound of the typewriter is not gay, it portends
always the next word coming, as if the experience
meant nothing in itself, & were only
for the sake of the words that it breeds, breeds like a
malarial swamp, old coasts of Sidney Lanier. Baktım baktım
says Turkish, I looked & looked, looked for the sound
& heard the swamp spread out towards sunset, mixed
my means & my measures, sprawled on my face in
an angry swarm of books. When the typewriter runs
I cant hear the rain in the drainpipe. When it rains
I cant hear it not raining. Should I complain?
Carry my nibbling anxiety up to the gate of a Castle
crying What am I to do with experience? It masters me!
It mans me & I weary of womaning it, of letting it plant
its seed in my head for me to take to the dictionary,
great treacherous swarming market, to sell in Balkh
what I bought in Bukhara, to sell in neat lines of order
what blew my head in as I would, now, blow in your gate.
The castle says Aldım, I took I got I received.
Can you silence the dictionary? Can you hear
the rain over the typewriter? I want reflection
brighter than source, that's why I used to like
lakes in New Hampshire, girls, traveling, grammars
of languages not spoken in Anudale. Appledale.
Rainspout, rainbarrel, tell me a rune,
tune louder than AC, righter than rain.

HOMAGE TO NIKOLAI ROERICH

That is to say behind the ice
white ice sharp pinnacles the sky is
dark blue as a tight new
pair of jeans worn in love's
unalterably fleshly mystery,
and a frozen waterfall steep
as a zipper tears open and behind
the hostile stiles of these mountains
a grand warm throbbing zone occurs
which I or any looker-on
would be pleased to enter—
right through the ogival cleft
to sink in country or draw out
depending on our needs an arm
capable of reaching inside us,
a wise arm, a wise warm hole—
beneath the ice the water cannot
be colder than its nature lets it
and in these mountains that
strikes me as warm, as red-hot
after that entropic cobalt sky.
He may have been too horny
even for a painter, he may have gone
too quickly in too much rapture
up the slope and down again
flailing those cold colors
after him, after all his heat
drained through those shining gaps.

EARTHBOUND

> Those ignorant, said Santayana,
> of the history of thought
> are doomed to re-enact it.

> *

> *Die Grenzen meiner Sprache*
> *bedeuten die Grenzen meiner Welt.*

> -Wittgenstein, *Tractatus* 5.6

Not bound .

      "the language is not bound"

but its own ways, muscles,
condyles,

    not bound.

      1.

There is a field
no grass deeper than ankle,
high cyclone fence & the dark
out of which two big dogs
came leaping, & that
they were on the far side
helped my thought not much.
I dont remember how we ever
got gas, got home,

          gone
into that night of fences
so dark even close to the
highway not one car passed.
Great Danes from the deep chest
shadows of them, heavy
footfalls past the fence
some moon. Roosevelt was gone
to sleep with Barbarossa & Charlie Chan.

The bombs we would never
understand came down & down
& I look down at my hands
knowing they are some part
or consequence of that time,
thirty years but the flesh
is supposed to change every seven,
my hands are & arent, hands,
what have they to do with it
it isnt a doing thing,
                  it says,
it is not bound, it has
nothing to do with me.
It happened & left me.
What I think about is or is not
helpful it is the only.
It is the only.

2.

Lately begun to circle over the higher field
its white underwings drenched with low sun
the hawk is not bound. It is not frequent

94

here but is not bound, is it,
it comes to prey upon the ground, it always
looks down,
            is it bound?

The time or ground or bond or band.
The bound.
            The time is ground
& bonds us to the
band of comrades the group the
individual to
            send below the yoke.
The company, Ted, the company
of our consciousness
yearns back from the river
as you & I are not, are not
wardens of those streams
hermetically close to our fields,
the North, the Androscoggin,
those ruin rivers.
            The company
yearns back from the hydraulic
aptitudes of
            "It is always modern times"
the time-bound (Korzybski)
                        time-binders
akasha
      our hands
    huddled, to make us, made us
the time or ground where we are bound.
This is Prometheus
his problem,
            Crimea, oranges
of Yalta, Chersonese,
                        long

hills between Euxine & Caspian,
sent under, we are sent under that yoke
stretched in the name of reality,
a river a band
                a bond man or bound.
Are veins, not arteries,
drain not supply. Are veins,
are bound.
            Bondi, the farmer
bound to his
                the link
is not elegant, endures.

                    3.

The company
to whom I am free
only in the minute
to sing heigh ho it is

bright sweet this
octobrine noon I sit
out back, Fall zephyrs
cool the heat of my balls

& oh, the cats go
up the hill beside
the young linden & the
Jonathan thought

flowering quince.
This freedom is my bond,
my word my boundary
I would break past

even against the chance
of contentment in this
eight-sided afternoon.
But I am bound

by the fact of the
company so are we all
to declare, that to speak
of music is "sentimentality"

but it is not I think
a quince it is some sort
of bred-back atavistic rose
of simple tooth-formula

pale pink & many thorns.
Yesterday the hawk flew
over it bound to the fall
to the ball of earth

summoning him down
from whatever teenage exploit
of his stubby, dactyl-
pointed bi-colored wings

down to eat & destroy
as is the order of act &
reflection at our membrane,
face of the word.

THE CONVECTIONS

for Helen

The convections
are under
I argue
order
or

muses
are meant
to be between
are close
are lost

The angle of Mars
anger of Mars
woke
to notice
what lay under

that under His body
lay a whirling
wheel
a simmer
in the endless ocean

the convections
are intimate
are close
the angles
curve

the anger turns
wide
of any mark
His lust
is continent

or arms
in secret
till He also
turns,
Mars

mourns
mourns also
the sea is sad
He knows
who knew it

blue "as ever"
to be true
to His lust
meant hurt
to His anger?

the angle turned
and opened
so that the sea
poured through
lay flat

the muse
that was Mars
He knew
Himself
in that alternative

99

element
He under
and lay down
to be healed
I am He

2.

Mars was more than a lord
of anger warcraft terror
Mars was more than a yard
shoved in Sabine loins:
Mars was mild

was earthly heat
trembled
at the end of the Valley
a shimmer
of His eyes

before His eyes
Mars
mind
meant more
a tenderness

was distance
and the distance
was so small or close
or loving or lovely
it touched

sometimes,
abolished
in the world
but never in the language
He never

forced, always
let the currents
kiss and dissever
or flow
or remember.

The distance
was His will to see to
touch and go
the closeness
was symmetrical

He woke at night
in the valley He was
to the warmth
of His seeing
senses

senses
generate
a thought
appals
the cool

air of phantasy
lulled Him
to a dream
where the agents
were of food

and compelled men to eat—
the dream left him
satisfied
He broke
His sleep

3.

The convections are under
and move what is over
the god is anger
that He be so moved
and not know it

or they are over
and are time
so that morrow
is slick
iridescent

where the convections
spill
up onto the beach
He awakened
to the colors

of change
the colors of order
He argued
sleep against
but slept

woke
of like mind
what is it
it moves
it moves by

it moves by the
slightest changes
it is the art
of prophecy
approximating

where He was
coming from
some homing
sense or care
was He

careful to maintain
the convections
are under
under and close
and never lost

because each wave
breaks
and by breaking
it renews,
knows

the past
and casts
it onward
shaped
like now

a little and then
mightily changed
He thought
by now
meant full Day.

4.

By slightest
(by sleight of?)
hands
the message
carries

tarries
only
in His ear
one·ly
the other

hard of
but He hears
the merest
(nearest?)
alternations

quarrels
of the ambient air
as if a name
were known
to call them

or they came.
They came to Him
knowing and showing
by slightest
differences

the world is made
He followed
aloud
and mapped
the intervals

as pores on His skin
so close and shapely
of like mind
produced
and saved

as treasure map
or portolan
against a morrow
shaped
just like today

and this skin
He loved
on Himself or Another
first text
He gave us

to look close
and take account
but dont count
sense
the margin

the cellular forward
or the precise
kiss
the touch!
the touch!

the convections
were how we knew
or He
out of ardor or anger
imposed

the image of His
approximations on
what covers me
this text this skin
this destiny.

5.

I see the crumbs
under the table
the long dull scar
below the sink
the dust

that is His war
cornered by air
conveyed into
and from this house
I see the glass

smeared with the
glazier's thumbprint
wall's white
shouldered buff
by the deed

or rough of passage,
I see the cat
facing east
from which a cool
wind is arriving

from which she came
an hour back
in from the chase
to catch
to catch!

is Mars and all
I see is pale today
and beautiful again
as if I had never
seen the like

before
the crumbs the scar
the pallid tawny
dry leaves of standing corn
stripped

for winter
I see a cloud
and things
keep coming back
shaped

shaped like each other
till the mind
balks
at the resemblance
and praise

god the differences
arise
newer than fire
and my eyes
categories

of all possible
dusts and fragments
one whole
enterprise
recommits

I am bidden
to this place
by the force
of my skin
and where

at its brightest
is eyes
for the difference
I also
can wake

as He did
enroll
in the company of morning
to control
my eyes!

are eyes equal
to the seen
or they exceed
the differences
in being same?

in being gold
they intimate
the audience
or seen,
in being

they arise
and I am guided
to the hill
up which the bare
trees stagger

all the differences
align
and we compose
our opposite
to be one

if it could be
again
or the first time
I hound no
matter

would not be
harder
than the particular
that the god
in being

made to be here
the cloud
the crumb the
philosophic dust
I wanted only

to be your lover
only
to renew
the implications
they were

my life
and I recovered
from my dream
to wake
in time

I thought
and thought again
the ardor
was increment
as the year went down

and the changeable
did change
and the dust
blew away
till I was left

alone
with the difference
in mind
and named it
You.

THE NAMES

Now the first flakes
now's tonight now's
night the flakes
as ever from the side
insinuate:
            into my bosom
come
come now my now
with a winter
            thicker than the merely militant
could understand,
            we for whom it was Love
so capitalized that
brought us here and appointed
pointed our noses to the Work

and this work is She
and this she is Thee upon whom
all our We have
emptied out the vials of their differences
as it seems,
            until you are You
simultaneous and full of glee
full of a glee called
Grace in the old texts
which also are entrusted to us
for our perusal,
            Maria von dem Schnee,
says H.D., Santa Maria de' Miracoli
one of those women

111

And who are those women? One speaks of them, saying their titles and relishing perhaps the fall of syllables that mark their names: Saaaaave, mocks Pound, Maria, saaaaave, the syllable of the hymn so pulled out. Maria, Miriam, Mariamne, Maria Prophetissa, Maria of Egypt, Black Virgin of the Egyptians called Gypsies/Yiftos/Tzigane/Romany/Tinkers, Black Virgin of the Old Language. What we celebrate under the names of such women (such a woman) is in fact the old language, older than Shelte and Lilith's runes, the old language embedded in all living languages, the grid before flesh to which flesh and speech are compatibly and confunctively obedient.

Mary, I ask, or name
meant now to be worshipped but then to be sung
at worst and at best
                         whispered into the beloved's ear
as since the War
one would say Helen, Helenê,
brought to the city (bedchamber, thalamos)
by Aphrodite.
              Who is herself
not the oldest of the gods, by far, but is,
she is, by far, the most
beautiful.

2.

What is to be remembered is the fall of breath
or how a man shudders caught
between the winter and the bedroom, her room,
to which he comes back hungry but often
such has the day been, reluctant
to turn his angers to such specific account
even where they will be most

112

annihilate and into sweetness flourish
given the companionable dark of her
instrument.
               Let him think of her so, of her so
equipped and mobilized in the penumbral bed
where he likes to find her but to which in fact
a last minute urgency has brought her
from the industrious hours when he is out there
a havering Someone past the marches of the house.
At any rate he finds her there, *welcoming* him
for Christ's sake, not even reluctant for his
transient intelligences and half-hearted news.
He knows nothing of the place she is.

3.

Such a matter it is to call out names, Isis, Mary, Helen,
Aphrodite,
               names of mothers
and unmothers, gay girls of male chauvinist cultures,
Ashera, Astarte, Ashtoreth,
her parts of shame distributed
as the vowels of her name.

               For every breath
               a shame,
               for every shame
               a mother of God.

               A name.
               Her parts
               are arts
               & still sustain us.

113

4.

What should I call you?
I vexed us both with the name & the finding
because of a dawning conviction
that to name the name is an obligation laid
on the old language to reveal itself.

And that unspoken name of God the rabbis
spell with four notes of music
would if sounded make
                    sound around us
the phonemic structure of the old speech
system by system unfolding into the clear
astronomy of life on earth, where from and how
to go, all things known or the structures
& locations of all things knowable. "Sung"
as they say or as they sing, the founded name
(or name found once again) begin.

THE ROAD TO CAPTREE

for Helen

Prepare the frame,
summon the picture to appear therein,
this straightedge road
to surround a linear experience.
Inside, right here,
where the bed frame is
set up the bed, boxspring, mattress,
headboard,
        set up a throb.
A wail. A yearning sob.
A whirl or whale
careened (turned over to show its
keel in day's air)
            on the strand,
show bottom on the beach, keel over hemline,
the road goes straight.

So remarkably. So surely the thin sunlight so cold
and later the vast moon over Carle Place,
craters & banners, hazes, rabbit, old man with faggots on his back,
La Luna,
        chaste
        in the heavy snow-threatened air.
Safely inland by that time, almost home, the light, the moon, oh
           the air
           forgives the moon
I said, meaning I forgive
           you for being beautiful.

At death to take away & Out that rhythm
the living know as breath

LES JOUEURS DE FOOT-BALL, 1908

(H. Rousseau)

Athletes come running up a field
held between tall trees.
The luminous ball
rises from hands or falls.

Most of the trees are lanced
with long elliptical cunnic holes.
The foliage is yellow
while the athletes hurry by.

My father is eight years old.
In nine years his brother Simon
will walk down this same glade.
There will be no flowers on the trees.

The young men who had been playing
have been eaten up by iron spheroids,
rhombic tanks, airplanes huzzahing
down on them like tantaluses

full of gallant agony. As Simon goes
a landmist of poison drifts to meet him.
Seeing it, for a moment he believes
the gas is soft blossoms on the trees,

the way they look now at evening,
corporeal light drifting through branches,
mustachioed young athletes moving towards me,
my father eight years old peers out from where he hides.

THE ENGINE DRIVER FIVE YEARS OLD

There is an ours outside of us,
a remembered necessity
that climbs down the daylight
as if it came to me
between the roses & the ivy,
an angel I knew as a door

door from the furnace room onto the garden.

That was the engine of the train I drove
fast towards the lilacs,
                    doorknob my throttle,
my breath the weather in the glass door.

At times I think I got there,
stepped down in a realm of pure color
such that flowers were roadsigns to it,

emissaries of the unfallen Day.

TO PERSEPHONE

for Helen

At morning read tracks embossed in grass,
        a message downward
to Persephone,
        all ready to melt this field
the snow goes.

        Rain that walks down empty trees,
tell her when you reach her house
how glibly she has been represented.
But that there still are men
who wait for her springtime,
        women who remember
& from the feel of their own bodies
intuit an arrival.

        From the way the light falls
it is impossible
to tell one patch of snow from itself melted
to a pool,
        both shimmer
near the tracks some drunken truck made

driving late last night in search of her too.

THE WILD BOY

The reclaimed child
brought out of the forest dreams
still the noiseless sunray, butterfly
                    riding down along it to the dark.

Why had words come?
What could they say
that had not been with him before,
reliable like water & fruit & pain?

The poem thinks of Kaspar Hauser or such like wolf or weirder children. First it sees a lovely soundless image, then the chatter of the world breaks in. Saying things. At first, it is just sad, that the flawless presence of the forest had been fouled by talk, contingency, insincerity, or sincerity itself, that rare fairweather friend. The last line mentions three things reliably sensuous. But the reader will recall times when fruit could not be counted on to be ripe or good, and when water has been brackish or doubtful. And will question the value of pain's dependability.

THE BEGUILING OF MERLIN

(Burne-Jones)

It is too soon to talk about love.

I think about children who show
their hidden parts & call it sex
that they are doing to each other.
Later love. Or it makes them pregnant
with a wilder child than they had ever been,
delivered from the forests of their loins
later, twelve to twenty, into the light.

No skin feels.
                    The cries of love
are locked below the social stone.
                              Taught there
with our own spells, lalage or agapology
of our soft sad lips.

                    1.

                    See his eyes, this Merlin,
as he is lured
busily exposing
his fatal mysteries
                    down into the pit,
          locked in time's honeycomb
                              humming
still to himself.

          I hear at the membrane,
stretched drum-head across cell-mouth,
how his song sums.

2.

What did they show, those spellbound children?
Their soft parts, folds & holds,
meek epopteia of the schoolyard
flashed into (how can it be?)
forever the life of the mind.
Later they would tell.
And then a fate like Merlin's
silences their secrecies.

3.

So the body, Body, later
is carried public
through a public world
to hide (yet be a sign of)
that private body of awed delight —

we grew into the rhythm of an active world
& lost in intercourse
the experimental science that brought us there.

We huddle for love's sake
now at the sonorous rock
beneath which Merlin groans
the explicit subtleties
he pays for with his life.
Rhythm is the stone that holds him down.

We see that in the snakes twining on Nimue's head,
cunning messengers she
lifted from him to adorn her thought —

or is it to confuse herself
back into the humbleness of first love
when her life felt him on her skin?

4.

She did love him once, I think.
And her power, against all her girlish
long ago expectations, her power
was exactly that she loved him.
How clear she is now, clarity
worked against charity, angry,
bitter-clear.

She loved him once, I think
she was a better lover ever than he.
Now her hips lock self-contained
self-containing around her ritual secrecy.

But for him, exhausted, behind her, beside her,
they lure him on
                    not meaning to.
He tells the last spell of his untouched mind.

5.

It's not the last word, a spell
is born every moment from the match
of the mind with its knowledge of itself,

its projected world. A spell
is born in heaven & rules in hell:
the sort of spell that locks

123

the mind's minder in a moment back,
seeing forever what he oncely saw.

He is trapped in how well he sees her.
How exhaustive his knowledge is
of all her goods & moods & movements!

It is only when the stone is down
his mind begins to touch her.

6.

Only when the last
spell is given
do the spells begin
that lead to heaven.

A bog & a big rock,
a temple
built in the mind
where he worships
the figure of her
dance lured in
around him
silencing
his desire in the
act of itself.

Bracketed between his crumpled body & her long
sex-denying form, a space opens
no more poignant than his depleted self-conscious eyes
that pity him for all the distances between.

A NATIVITY

The magic forest
through which the wisemen come
aghast at the smallness
of this anointed one
they've half imagined.

Their journey
seems to have taken all their lives
to come to the center of some woods
where a child is born
in the lovely dappled shade of matter

but not touched by it.
The woods go on.

VENUS VERTICORDIA

(Rossetti)

Not a mouth or eyes made familiar from canvas to canvas, part then of our family. Instead, she shows the unexpected, precise, left breast. Towards it the undulant bronze dart points, as if she meant to wound hereself and make herself hopelessly in love with her beholder. Because of that flame of alloy in her hand, she is or soon will be in love with my eyes, eyes that are themselves wounded to love by the sight or prospect of her self-wound. That she would fall from herself into love makes me love her. Without that expectation, where would love be? She means, I mean, that strange old sort of love wherein to enter one must 'fall'.

e been that he was near death.

reign languages became
lerstand.

felt, looking at the Greek
liad,

d in fact read there
urning around a war,

rittle in the sky
a fine full moon.

consolation,
or riding a bicycle.

ld understand
eople werent talking

dmired a shapely young
ng out of a car

& was suddenly overcome with her grief
even before he saw the sick

little girl she helped out, & the bleak
doctor's doorway beyond the Plymouth.

Her shape told me she was sad,
he thought, & then he allowed his thought

to make love to her & her sadness both
while he drove up the highway towards

it *must* be death it is so empty & so kind.

ORPHEUS

spirits of the
or the animals themselves
dazzling his eyes before
the unkempt
garden of his thoughts he
wandered lost
his song his song uncurled
around the dew-sick vines
rot into intricacy where

a drink for this god was
oozing into
the cup he took for his head
his brain he also thought it
the dapple on the surface of
the surface the surface the
song the song

"I am held back
every mortal night
from a decisive act I yearn
every part of me to
do it simple
be it simple
be it so simple not even

squirrels & the dryads could more"
but one edge of praise
lingered in him
like the taste of an animal he

had long ago killed eaten
half-become

                this praise
knew some other
destination
chained him
to an austere hypothesis
aching he felt it aching
past the web of the wood.

                      2.

Song: not a thing
to listen to
but by an old convention
the faculty to arouse
things & speech
to a musical condition
drifting outward
from the singer
into the mysterious poise
so long maintained
between north & south poles,

his song then,
or power to follow
the musical gestures
of his chosen
vocabulary
his companions
down into the forest
of their nonce connections
& out to the Pure Crystal

Fountains where

where something happened
or had once happened
sudden as an indian raid
& even longer ago,
something bursting
out of the song
& putting clothes on say
walking around

the renewable vegetation
of this strange place.
Period.
For the longest time
he thought song
would teach causality
& thus by magic
roll back effects
into the flagrant potency
from which an act

had
(maybe)
uncoiled them.
Not so.   The song
was parabolic, perimetric,
sang about itself,
causal even
though not about cause.
Then he supposed
this very garden or planet
had been changed into
Being.
Was this Being?

He relied
on etymology,
the chant sufficed,
the diseased chickens
hurried across
any number of roads
magicked
to bring fertility
or its cross
cousin Opposite
into the yam-yard
of all our Neighbors

surely.   Or not so
surely but quickly
at least. He followed
his capacity
to arouse
chickens & oakleaves
to predictable
beautiful
Dispositions

per musicam
i.e., by his faculty
and so forth
to sway, yea
rocks & stocks &
economic agriculture
danced at his behest
or hest or
was it His
at all
or hers, Hers,
he thought

surely it's Hers.
After all
it was She
whose Hers
had empowered his
His for a while then
withdrew the environment
whooosh from which
& in which only the struck
notes of his phorminx
could sound
in the not noticeably
golden air of late autumn,

always the chanciest time
I knew or I know
She said to Him to say
he said it & meant
to be still
I mean quiet soundless still
on barbitos & phorminx & fender
tortoise & piba & claves
Ecuadorian panpipes
& the late Admiral Yama-
moto's long lost shakuhachi
singing from the bottom of the sea

aieee or aiooo
we have achieved
you & I
an enviable condition
call Recency
known in acute stages as Now
where his music
summms around your partials

& resolves
what had never even once
been risked

he risks now!
Song is Risk
I rede you,
Song's risk
& no light's
lighter
no tune truer

than loses
itself in
itself
by day or by
night always
telling &
telling

sweet thee
& deft me
to ride
when the
Point
blossoms
into everywhere.

3.

I yield my freedom
to have known you,

you lady dim

in the interstices
of a lost network
leading out of time,

old radio broadcasts
back from the nebulae
back from the
Moon, Lady
                vague
as the moon
must be understood
to have been
before an outpost
of our enerty
becomes she,

                Lady
integrable
with my needs I abash
before the selfish
will of my will,
my vajra vigor
claims you my
songs understand you—

"Them?
I have heard
those programs before,
baked in sunday childhood boring
as before,
nonetheless I rise to you
along the Avenue of Dogs
the clement ever clement
weather of late Hell

to attend your
noises,
            never
hope to see me

as I am."

Printed February 1978 in Santa Barbara & Ann Arbor
for the Black Sparrow Press by Mackintosh and Young
& Edwards Brothers Inc. Design by Barbara Martin.
This edition is published in paper wrappers; there
are 250 hardcover copies numbered & signed by the
author; & 50 numbered copies have been handbound in
boards by Earle Gray each containing an original
holograph poem by the author.

Robert Kelly was born in 1935 in Brooklyn. Since 1961 he has published thirty or more books and pamphlets, most of them poetry, a few prose. *The Convections* is his first large collection of poems in several years, following *The Mill of Particulars* (1973) and *The Loom* (1975). Robert Kelly teaches at Bard College, and lives with his wife Helen in Annandale.